For The Love of

Shakespeare

K. B. Chandra Raj

Order this book online at www.trafford.com
or email orders@trafford.com

Most Trafford titles are also available at major online book retailers.

Printed in the United States of America.

ISBN: 978-1-4269-6802-0 (sc)
ISBN: 978-1-4269-6803-7 (hc)
ISBN: 978-1-4269-6804-4 (e)

Library of Congress Control Number: 2011907050

Trafford rev. 05/05/2011

 www.trafford.com

North America & international
toll-free: 1 888 232 4444 (USA & Canada)
phone: 250 383 6864 ♦ fax: 812 355 4082

For Neela and Deeran:

Because of whom doting grandparents from three continents will always be around.

"He that tries to recommend (Shakespeare) by select quotations will succeed like the pedant in "Hierocles", who, when he offered his house to sale, carried a brick in his pocket as a specimen."

Samuel Johnson.

Why Shakespeare?

All religions make this simple plea: Love one another. And religion in one form or another has existed from the beginning of time. Mahatma Gandhi, Martin Luther King, Mandela and that unflappable and serene Aung San Suu Kyi among others practiced what Christ preached; the saintly Mother Theresa neck-deep in the trenches of poverty, sickness and squalor worked her heart out to alleviate suffering; theologian, philosopher, model teacher, Thomas Aquinas had a profound influence on the Catholic Church.

They all made this world a better place but failed where the English language succeeded – to bring people of disparate cultures from different countries with diverse aspirations, together. From the banks of the Ganges to sacred Lourdes in the foot hills of the Pyrenees; from Freetown in West Africa to Murcia in East of Spain; from Seoul to Shanghai you can get by armed with knowledge of English. One man who will always remain front and center of this much sought after universal medium; the greatest name in the English language is Shakespeare. Sophocles, Tolstoy, Twain, Plutarch, Dickens, Hans Christian Anderson are all bright stars in the literary galaxy but the brightest of them all, the lode star, is William Shakespeare.

Shakespeare told every kind of story – comedy, tragedy, adventure, love stories, fairy tales, melodrama and many more. During the time the Globe Theater remained burned down he switched to writing sonnets, the likes of which have yet to be seen.

Who will not be moved by the wisdom and music in these lines?

*"Like as the waves make towards the pebbled shore,
So do our minutes hasten to their end."
*"But if the while I think on thee, dear friend,
All losses are restored and sorrows end."
*"Who having two sweet babes, when death takes one,
Will slay the other and be nurse to none."
*Who buys a minute's mirth to wail a week?
Or sells eternity to get a toy?
For one sweet grape who will the vine destroy?"

To the question "Why Shakespeare?" author Harold Bloom succinctly provided the answer in four words. "Who else is there?"

You may ask, "What qualifies you to comment on Shakespeare?"

The answer can be found in these questions.

Does one have to sculpt a David like Michelangelo or sketch like Toulouse-Lautrec the Can-Can dancers of the Moulin Rouge to be awed by the majesty and beauty of the human form?

Do we not all lose ourselves in admiration witnessing a figure skater completing a Triple Axel Jump?

Don't children and adults alike hold their breaths in disbelief during a flying trapeze act when the flyer and catcher with complete control of muscle and mind, after doing twists and turns, flying and catching in midair return "home" safely?

Pray, does one have to be able to duplicate the feats of Hank Aaron or Babe Ruth the "Sultan of Swat", to be dazzled by the coordination, timing and lightning speed with which a triple play in Base Ball is executed?

What will you find within the covers?

Familiar Expressions.

While looking over the books on the third floor of our town's library, "One Hundred Best One-Liners" by Jack W. Thomas caught my attention. Below each 'One-liner' he also had words used in Shakespeare's plays which have become house hold expressions. There must certainly be many more I thought. How about his sonnets? There must be some there too. And so patiently and sometimes painfully, ('Good Heavens, Why do I need to do this?') I labored through Shakespeare's plays, his sonnets, 'The Rape of Lucrece' and 'Adonis' and extracted expressions which we all use innocent of the fact they were either Shakespeare's own invention or made popular by him. When for instance a young man is referred to as "A Romeo" even in the remotest village on the globe it is understood right away that he is a young man in love.

Every time I fact -checked my work I came across new familiar expressions. One cannot empty the Atlantic Ocean with a tea cup. Like the Horn of Plenty the plays and poems keep on giving. It is believed well educated English speaking people use generally around five thousand words but in Shakespeare's plays we come across as many as eighteen thousand different words. That is the genius of Shakespeare.

It must be mentioned that the English language like the vast ocean receives its sustenance from all sources. Words from non-English speaking countries have found their way into the English language; 'pundit' and 'karma' from Sanskrit, 'hamburger' from German, 'admiral' from French, 'hacienda' from Spanish, 'haiku' and 'kabuki' from Japanese, Brooklyn (Breukelen), Blunderbuss(Donderbus) and Booze(Busen) from the Dutch to name just a few.

Malapropisms and even gaffes like Sarah Palin's "Refudiate" have sneaked in. Only that final arbiter Father Time can tell us whether new words will have the same staying power as those of Shakespeare's expressions that have become household words or end up merely "One Night Delights", here to-night gone tomorrow.

Familiar Expressions in context.

When I first came across the expression "Cabined, cribbed, confined" I liked it. The alliteration, the rhythm and beat in that line expressing in physical terms a mental state got my attention. I was not aware it was from Macbeth until I read the play. To appreciate and truly understand the appropriateness of the expression one must know the circumstances that impel Macbeth to utter them.
Macbeth on the urgings of his ambitious wife murders his kinsman and king, Duncan, who was visiting him to honor his valor in battle. From this point on Macbeth is weighed down by guilt – "Then comes my fit again: I had else been perfect, whole as a marble, founded as the rock, as broad and general as the casing air: **But now I am cabined, cribbed, confined,** bound in to saucy doubts and fears.." In Hamlet Shakespeare advises, "Suit the action to the word, the word to the action." We see it in action in this instance.

Do these expressions from Shakespeare's plays and poems, now over four hundred years old, mean the same today? The best way to ascertain that is to place them in context as they appear in the plays and poems. I have selected a few popular expressions and presented them just as they appear in the text.

My conclusion is that except for random exceptions, they mean the same today as they were deigned over four hundred years ago.

The Quintessential Shakespeare.

My work is totally subjective. Be it a painting, a poem or a song, each one of us reacts to them differently; some even indifferently. While reading Shakespeare I came across passages I could not pass by. I felt I had to record it. The words had the sound of music and always making sound sense. This may not be your 'quintessential' Shakespeare. I hope you will enjoy reading them all the same. If ten Rolls Royce cars, "The Silver Shadow" all of them, are lined up and I am asked to pick one, how would I go about it? Well may be I will go for the color. That's how I felt in selecting the passages.

Short Bites from Shakespeare.

"What the aristocratic writers get for free from nature, intellectuals of lower birth have to pay with their youth" – **Anton Chekov writing to a friend.**
We have heard it said with perhaps a sprinkling of sarcasm and a pinch of envy that the Bushes, patricians all, father and children were 'born on third base'; that they did not have to strive for anything. President Bush was tarred publicly during the Katrina crisis, "He does not care for black people." Understandably wealthy people by and large tend to be insensitive to the sufferings of the less fortunate because they cohort mostly and most of the time with the affluent. How do the rest respond to tragedies like Katrina, Tsunami and Darfur? They wipe their consciences clean with a check hastily written and hurriedly mailed and move on. The thrust of what I mean to say is that no two people can be expected to think and feel alike. And, certain experiences cannot be communicated. Could a woman ever be able to explain to a man the emotional calisthenics she goes through prior to and during child birth? It has to be experienced. Shakespeare sums up all that I have labored to

communicate in just one line. **"He jests at scars that never felt a wound."**

When communicating we all want to grab the attention of the listener. These **Short Bites** are fresh expressions when woven into conversations, writings and speeches can be effective in perking the interest of the listener. We have heard it said many times the job being too much for Mister Exe and it brought him down – "He could not cope"
"The hind that would be mated by the lion must die for love."

Shakespeare, His women and I.

"Do you know madam Ducoudary, it has never occurred to me to read Shakespeare? Sheer ingratitude, madam. We women above all should make a cult of him. Because he has created the most admirable examples of our sex. Juliet, Miranda, Desdemona, Perdita are types of women we must all admire."
That from Alexander Dumas's absorbing novel, "Fernande"
"Good god" I screamed internally. How true. Shakespeare may have been for all I know the first suffragette.
And so I went back for a second bite with gusto.
I googled to see whether there is any literature on this. "By Gad", There were as you and I would say "tons"; but none in my home town library. I requested they kindly get me what I fancied by way of the inter library loan arrangement. As always competent, courteous and co -operative, at least five books came tumbling in, in double quick succession.
I thumbed through them all and was disappointed. They were all highfalutin, very erudite, very intellectual, and very cerebral - tediously didactic. About patriarchal society, male dominated society, the submissiveness of women and on and on. "I might as well read the stock market report in the Wall Street Journal; who's up; who's down " I growled. All this pontification and pedantry about male domination I mused when a woman was at this time ruling England

- Queen Elizabeth, a Queen who engineered the humiliating defeat of the Spanish Armada. I have had it up to here.

I decided I should write not from the top of my head but rather from the pit of my stomach. Get back to reading the play itself. "Play's the thing." Read, reflect and record. I did not see these women as second strings. On the contrary on many occasions they outsmarted and eclipsed the men. I found them caring, faithful, pretty, smart, sensuous, and scheming. If it were not so, Shakespeare will be a period playwright and not one for all time as he is. I was happy to read this line from Nobel Laureate Aleksandr Solzhenitsyn's Nobel Prize acceptance speech. "It is in vain to affirm that which the heart does not confirm."

I focus on women in a few plays to present my case. Not by the broad brush of a house painter but instead by the surgeon's selective use of the sanitized scalpel.

The power of Shakespeare's words.

During the time of Shakespeare (1565-1616) plays were staged in the raw. By this I mean there was no lighting, performances were held during the day, in open air, hampered by poor acoustics; no attention grabbing screens and sophisticated props of the modern stage. The actors had to constantly compete for attention with the voluble, lackadaisical groundlings (penny ticket holders) in the pit – standing room only; vendors selling food and drink all going on simultaneously.

There was no fourth wall as we know it today. In this environment to get through to the audience the playwright had to almost entirely depend on the power of words and the ability of the players to enunciate them effectively. They have to be heard over the din and cacophony in the pit.

Shakespeare began, continued and ended his career in the theater as an actor. He related life to the stage and acting - **"All the world's a stage", "Life's but a walking shadow, a poor player that struts**

and frets upon the stage, and then is heard no more." He knew he had a problem of being heard. He therefore packed his plays with the power of words and had the players communicate them forcefully. Many of his speeches he assigned to his characters were specially written to be spoken loudly even shouted. Imagine a line like **"FRIENDS, ROMANS, COUNTRYMEN"** being whispered to a rambunctious, rabble, many of whom had never been to school and heckled actors whom they disliked.

Contrast this environment with what takes place today. No taking of pictures; no recordings to be done; all cell phones must be put away; patrons not permitted to cavalierly enter and exit at will. The appeal before the lights go dim, "You may take this time to unwrap your lozenges" is a polite reminder, albeit with a smack of levity to please remain silent for the duration of the play.

It was only in 1623 seven years after Shakespeare's death that these plays appeared in print. This meant if you missed something you have missed it for good unless you go back the second time. The patron had to therefore listen closely to the words and form his own impression.

Cleopatra is described thus:
"The barge she sat in, like a burnished throne,
Burned on the water: the poop was beaten gold;
Purple the sails, and so perfumed that
The winds were love-sick with them….
For her own person, it beggared all description."

I have selected a few prominent men and women in Shakespeare's plays whose personalities come through from the words they utter. By their words they shall be judged.

Confessions:

*My heartfelt thanks to Siva my loving wife, who tirelessly, whole heartedly and in good humor affords me the luxury of leisure and for prepping me with the necessary logistical wherewithal without which this project would not have gone beyond the realm of good intentions.

*My sincere thanks to the friendly staff at the Whitneyville Branch of the Hamden Library System for suffering my presence every day and for creating for all patrons a congenial environment - for adults to work upstairs and for kids to play downstairs.

*The Bard and I share a dubious distinction. We both never saw the inside of a university. The similarity ends there.

*I have had no formal training in English literature, much less in Shakespeare. Call me an autodidact if you will.

*This work was researched, fact checked, collated and edited entirely by me. Self-editing can be a tricky business akin to a dentist drilling his own teeth. Any errors of omission or commission are my own making. I ask the reader for his or her understanding and forbearance.

* I am greatly indebted to my childhood pal Dr. Sid Perinpanayagam for encouraging me to undertake this project and for his wise counsel.

*I have imagined the reader of this book to be a person already acquainted in one degree or another with the poems and plays of Shakespeare. Readers will observe the format of this product does not conform to the traditional mold. I decided to do it my way.

K.B.ChandraRaj
Hamden, Connecticut.
September 16, 2010.

Familiar Expressions

From the title of Shakespeare's plays

Measure for Measure

The Comedy of Errors

Much Ado about Nothing

Love's Labor's Lost

All's Well That Ends Well

From Shakespeare's plays

Antony and Cleopatra

My salad days.   Act1. Scene5.
Beggar'd all description.   Act2. Scene2.
Love-sick.   Act2. Scene2.

Her infinite variety.   Act2. Scene2.

Long lost friends.   Act 4. Scene12.

King Henry 1V. Part.1

Give the devil his due. Act1. Scene2.

Loose behavior. Act1. Scene2.

The game is afoot. Act1. Scene3.

Stony-hearted villains. Act2. Scene2.

As merry as crickets. Act2. Scene4.

Send him packing. Act2. Scene4.

Set my teeth on edge. Act3. Scene1.

Tell truth and shame the devil. Act3. Scene1.

Dog his heels. Act3. Scene2.

The better part of valor is discretion. Act 5 Scene 4.

Henry 1V Part 11

Eaten me out of house and home.   Act2. Scene1.

Small beer.   Act2. Scene2.

Uneasy lies the head that wears a crown.   Act3. Scene1.

King Henry V

Devils incarnate. Act2. Scene3.

Once more unto the breach, dear friends, once more.   Act3. Scene1.

Heart-string.   Act4. Scene1.

We band of brothers.   Act4.   Scene3.

Household words.   Act4. Scene3.

King Henry V1. Part 1

Here, there, and every where.   Act1. Scene1.

Hare-brained.   Act1. Scene2.

Halcyon days.   Act1.   Scene2.

Fight till the last gasp.   Act1.   Scene2.

King Henry V1. Part. 11

Let's kill all the lawyers. Act4. Scene2.

As dead as a doornail. Act4. Scene10.

Heart turned to stone. Act 5. Scene 2.

King Henry V1. Part 111

Breathed his last.   Act5. Scene2.

Friend or foe. Act 5. Scene 2.

Sprung like summer flies. Act 2. Scene 6.

King Henry V111

For goodness' sake.   Prologue.

Othello

We cannot all be masters.   Act1. Scene1.

Heaven is my judge.   Act1. Scene1.

Lined their coats.   Act1. Scene1.

Wear my heart upon my sleeve. Act1. Scene1.

Who steals my purse steals trash. Act3. Scene3.

The green-eyed monster.   Act3. Scene3.

Pride, pomp and circumstance. Act3. Scene3.

Whistle her off.   Act3. Scene3.

Of one that loved not wisely but too well. Act5. Scene2.

Led by the nose. Act 1. Scene 3.

Womb of time. Act1. Scene 3.

Twelfth Night

If music be the food of love, play on. Act1. Scene1.

Some are born great, some achieve greatness
And some have greatness thrust upon them.   Act2. Scene5.

Laugh yourselves into stitches. Act3. Scene2.

Out of the jaws of death. Act3. Scene4.

Love's Labor's Lost

Money's worth. Act2. Scene1.

Sweet hearts. Act5. Scene2.

One word in secret. Act5. Scene2.

Razor's edge. Act5. Scene2.

To show his teeth. Act5. Scene2.

The apple of her eye. Act5. Scene2.

Troilus and Cressida

A good riddance. Act2. Scene1.

Snail-paced. Act5. Scene5.

As You Like It

Laid on with a trowel. Act1. Scene2.

In a better world than this. Act1. Scene2.

This working day-world. Act1. Scene3.

Sweet are the uses of adversity. Act2. Scene1.

All the world's a stage. Act2. Scene7.

We have seen better days. Act2. Scene7.
Bag and baggage. Act3. Scene2.

Too much of a good thing. Act4. Scene2.

Will not kill a fly. Act4. Scene2.

Good wine needs no bush. Epilogue.

Macbeth

Fair is foul, and foul is fair. Act1. Scene1.

The milk of human kindness. Act1. Scene5.

Unsex me here. Act1. Scene5.

The be-all and end-all. Act1. Scene7.

Poisoned chalice. Act1. Scene7.

Even-handed justice. Act1. Scene7.

Fatal vision. Act2. Scene1.

There's no such thing. Act2. Scene1.

Knock, Knock, Knock. Who's there
in the name of Beelzebub. Act2. Scene3.

Roast your goose. Act2. Scene3.

What's done is done. Act3. Scene2.

Cabined, cribbed, confined. Act3. Scene4.

Cut-throat. Act3. Scene 4.

The crack of doom. Act4. Scene1.

At one fell swoop. Act4. cene3.

Full of sound and fury. Act5. Scene5.

All our yesterdays. Act5. Scene5.

Hamlet

Not a mouse stirring.   Act1. Scene1.

That it should come to this. Act1. Scene2.

In my mind's eye.   Act 1 Scene 2.

Frailty, thy name is woman. Act1. Scene2.

More in sorrow than in anger. Act1. Scene2.

To thine own self be true. Act1. Scene3.

The primrose path.   Act1. Scene3.

Neither a borrower nor a lender be. Act1. Scene3.

To the manner born.   Act1. Scene4.

More honored in the breach than the observance. Act. 1. Scene 4.

Something is rotten in the state of Denmark. Act1. Scene4.

Murder most foul. Act1. Scene5.

The time is out of joint. Act. 1. Scene 5.

There are more things in heaven and earth, Horatio,
than are dreamt of in your philosophy.   Act1. Scene5.

One may smile, and smile, and be a villain. Act1. Scene5.

Here's my drift. Act2. Scene1.

Brevity is the soul of wit. Act2. Scene2.

Words, words, words. Act2. Scene2.

What a piece of work is a man. Act2. Scene2.

Hamlet

Pigeon-livered. Act2. Scne2.

Though this be madness, yet there's method in it. Act2. Scene2.

The play's the thing. Act2. Scene2.

An old man is twice a child. Act2. Scene2.

The slings and arrows. Act3. Scene1.

The whips and scorns. Act. 3. Scene 1.

There's the rub. Act3. Scene1.

To be, or not to be. Act3. Scene1.

Sea of troubles. Act3. Scene1.

Get thee to a nunnery. Act. 3. Scene 1.

Conscience does make cowards of us all. Act3. Scene1.

The law's delay. Act3. Scene1.

Sugar O'er. Act3. Scene1.

God has given you one face,
and you make yourselves another.   Act3. Scene1.

Trippingly on the tongue.   Act3. Scene2.

The very witching time of night.   Act. 3. Scene 2.

Suit the action to the word.   Act. 3. Scene 2.

In my heart of heart.   Act. 3. Scene 2.

To feed and clothe.   Act. 3. Scene 2.

O, woe is me.   Act. 3. Scene 2.

The lady doth protest too much, me thinks.   Act. 3. Scene 2.

Hamlet

Wash it white as snow. Act3. Scene3.

It smells to heaven. Act3. Scene3.

Black as death. Act3.Scene 3.

Wring your heart.   Act. 3. Scene 4.

Hoist with his own petard.   Act3. Scene4.

I must be cruel, only to be kind.   Act. 3. Scene 4.

When sorrows come, they come not in single spies,
but in battalions.   Act. 4. Scene 5.

Ministering angel.   Act. 5. Scene 1.

The cat will mew and dog will have his day.   Act. 5. Scene 1.

Sweets to sweet. Act5. Scene1.

There's a divinity that shapes our ends. Act5. Scene2.

A towering passion.   Act. 5. Scene 2.

Flights of angels sing thee to thy rest. Act. 5. Scene 2.

The rest is silence. Act5. Scene2.

The readiness is all. Act. 5. Scene 2.

King Lear

Although the last, not the least.   Act. 1. Scene 1.

Nothing will come out of nothing.   Ac1. 1. Scene 1.

My heart into my mouth.   Act. 1. Scene 1.

Sharper than a serpent's tooth it is,
to have a thankless child.   Act1. Scene5.

I am a man more sinned against than sinning. Act. 3. Scene 2.

Every inch a king.   Act. 4. Scene 6.

Who loses and who wins; who's in, who's out. Act. 5. Scene 3.

Tell old tales. Act5. Scene3.

Shut your mouth, dame,
Or, with this paper shall I stop it.

The Merchant of Venice

The devil can cite Scripture for his purpose.   Act1. Scene2.

Truth will out. Act2. Scene2.

In the twinkling of an eye.   Act2. Scene2.

Hold a candle to. Act2. Scene6.

All that glisters is not gold. Act. 2. Scene 7.

My torch bearer. Act2. Sceene7.

The quality of mercy. Act. 4. Scene 1.

A Daniel come to judgment. Act. 4. Scene1.

A pound of flesh.   Act. 4. Scene 1.

Swan-like end. Act 3. Scene 2.

Let me play the fool. Act1. Scene1.

Snail-slow. Act 2. Scene 5.

Romeo and Juliet

Star-crossed lovers. Prologue.

What's in a name?   Act. 2. Scene 2.

Parting is such sweet sorrow.   Act2. Scene2.

Wild-goose chase.   Act. 2. Scene 4.

The law on my side. Act. 2. Scene 4.

A fool's paradise. Act. 2. Scene 4.

A plague on both your houses. Act. 3. Scene 1.

O, I am fortune's fool. Act. 3. Scene 1.

The Tempest

Sea-change.   Act1. Scene2.

What's past is prologue. Act. 2. Scene 1.

Strange-bedfellow.   Act. 2. Scene 2.

Virgin-knot. Act. 4. Scene 1.

We are such stuff as dreams are made on. Act. 4. Scene 1.

Melted into air. Act. 4. Scene 1.

O brave new world. Act. 5. Scene 1.

In this pickle. Act. 5. Scene 1.

Watch-dogs. Act 1. Scene 2.

Swim like a duck. Act 3. Scene 1.

Brain him. Act 3. Scene 2.

Chanticleer cry cock-a-diddle-doo.   Act 1. Scene 2.

Give a doit (coin of little worth) Act 2. Scene 2.

Julius Caesar

Beware the ides of March. Act1. Scene2.

Lean and hungry look. Act. 1. Scene 2.

Like a Colossus. Act. 1. Scene 2.

Done to death by slanderous tongues. Act1. Scene2.

It was Greek to me. Act. 1. Scene 3.

Fit for the gods. Act. 2. Scene 1.

Never stood on ceremonies. Act. 2. Scene 2.

Cowards die many times before their deaths. Act. 2. Scene 2.

Et tu, Brute. Act. 3. Scene 1.

Constant as the northern star. Act. 3. Scene 1.

The dogs of war. Act. 3. Scene 1.

Tide of times. Act3. Scene1.

Lend me your ears. Act. 3. Scene 2.

And Brutus is an honorable man. Act. 3. Scene 2.

O, what a fall was there, my country men. Act. 3. Scene 2.

Unkindest cut of all. Act. 3. Scene 2.

An itching palm. Act. 4. Scene 3.

There is a tide in the affairs of men. Act. 4. Scene 3.

The Comedy of Errors

Neither rhyme nor reason. Act. 2. Scene 2.
There is something in the wind. Act. 3. Scene 1.

King Richard 11

Spotless reputation. Act1. Scene1.

King Richard 111

The winter of our discontent. Act. 1. Scene 1.

Make a short shrift. Act. 3. Scene 4.

A horse, a horse, my kingdom for a horse. Act. 5. Scene 4.

Cymbeline

The game is up.　Act. 3. Scene 3.

I have not slept one wink.　Act. 3. Scene 4.

Sweet words. Act 5. Scene 3.

The Merry Wives of Windsor

Eye-wink.　Act. 2. Scene 2.

The world's mine oyster.　Act. 2. Scene 2.

This is the short and long of it.　Act. 2. Scene 2.

Throw cold water.　Act. 2. Scene 3.

Laughing-stocks.　Act. 3. scene 1.

The Winter's Tale

As white as driven snow.　Act. 4. Scene 4.

The Taming of the Shrew

Have a stomach to it. Act. 1. Scene 2.

Break the ice. Act1. Scene 2.

A little pot and soon hot. Act. 4. Scene 1.

A way to kill a wife with kindness. Act. 4. Scene 1.

For ever and a day. Act. 4. Scene 4.

The Two gentlemen Of Verona

Invisible as a nose on a man's face,
or a weathercock on a steeple. Act. 2. Scene 1.

To make a virtue of necessity. Act. 4. Scene 1.

King John

Play fast and loose. Act. 3. Scene 1.

As tedious as a twice-told tale. Act. 3. Scene 4.

To paint the lily. Act. 4. Scene 2.

Make haste, the better foot before. Act. 4. Scene 2.

Coriolanus

Death by inches. Act. 5. Scene 4.

Much Ado About Nothing

As merry as the day is long. Act. 2. Scene 1.

Lie low. Act. 5. Scene 1.

Done to death. Act. 5. Scene 3.

A Midsummer Night's Dream

Swift as a shadow. Act 1. Scene 1.

Fancy-free. Act. 2. Scene 1.

King Richard 111

In Gods, name: Act1. Scene1V.

From Shakespeare's poems

Venus and Adonis

Bold-faced.

Hard as steel.

Owl, night's herald.

Blood doth boil.

And so to so.

Licking of his wound.

Cold terror.

Lily white.

Next of blood.

The Rape of Lucrece

Swift and short.

One for all, or all for one.

Blows the smoke of it into his face.

Dead of night.

Watch-word.

High - treason.

Lode-star.

Soul and body.

Sonnets

Wide-world. XX1X

Curse my fate. XX1X.

Remembrance of things past. X X X

My eye doth feast. X LV 11.

Heavy eye lids. L X 1

Edge of doom: C X V 1.

More or less: C X X 111.

I am that I am. CXX1.

Raven black. C X X V 11

To boot. C X X X V.

Better Angel. C X L1V

As gently day doth follow night. CX LV.

As black as hell, as dark as night.   CXLV11.

Familiar Expressions in Context

My salad days:
Cleopatra:
My salad days,
When I was green in judgment: cold in blood,
To say as I did then. But, come, away;
Get me ink and paper:
He shall have every day a several greeting,
Or I'll unpeople Egypt.
Antony and Cleopatra.

Eaten me out of house and home.
Chief Justice: How now, Sir John. What are you brawling here?
Doth this become your place, your times and business?
You should have been well on your way to York.
Stand from him fellow: Wherefore hang'st upon him?
Hostess: O my most worshipful lord, an't please
Your grace, I am a poor widow of Eastcheap, and
He is arrested at my suit.
Chief Justice: For what sum?
Hostess: It is more than for some, my lord;
It is for all, all I have. **He hath eaten me out of house
 And home:** he hath put all my substance into that fat
 Belly of his: but I will have some of it out again,
Or I will ride thee O' nights like the mare.
Henry 1V Part 11.

Uneasy lies the head that wears the crown.
King: How many thousand of my poorest subjects
Are at this hour asleep. O sleep, O gentle sleep,
Nature's soft nurse, how have I frighted thee,
That thou no more wilt weigh my eye lids down
And sleep my senses in forgetfulness? …..
O thou dull god, why liest thou with the vile
In loathsome beds, and leavest the kingly couch
A watch-case or a common 'larum- bell?...
Canst thou, O partial sleep, give thy repose
To the wet sea-boy in an hour so rude,
And in the calmest and most stillest night,
With all appliances and means to boot,
Deny it to a king? Then happy low, lie down.
Uneasy lies the head that wears a crown.
Henry 1V. Part 11.

Once more unto the breach.
The game's afoot.
King Henry: **Once more unto the breach,**
 Dear friends, once more;
Or close the wall up with our English dead….
For there is none of you so mean and base
That hath not noble luster in your eyes.
I see you stand like greyhounds in the slips,
Straining upon the start. **The game's afoot:**
Follow your spirit, and upon this charge
Cry 'God for Harry, England, and Saint George '
 King Henry V

Band of Brothers.
We few, we happy few, we **band of brothers:**
For he to-day that sheds his blood with me
Shall be my brother; be he never so vile,
This day shall gentle his condition:
And gentlemen in England now a-bed
Shall think themselves accursed they were not here,
And hold their manhoods cheap whiles any speaks
That fought with us upon Saint Crispin's day.
King Henry V.

The first thing we do, let's kill all the lawyers.
Cade: I thank you, good people: there shall be no money;
All shall eat and drink on my score; and I will apparel them
All in one livery, that they may agree like brothers and worship
Me their lord.
Dick: **The first thing we do, let's kill all the lawyers.**
Cade: Nay that I mean to do. Is not this a lamentable thing,
That of the skin of an innocent lamb should be made a parchment?
That parchment, being scribbled over, should undo a man?
Some say the bee stings: but I say, 'tis the bee's wax; for
I did but steal once to a thing, and I was never mine own man since.
Henry V1. Part11.

Who steals my purse steals trash.
Iago: Good name in a man and woman, dear my lord,
Is the immediate jewel of their souls;
Who steals my purse steals trash; 'tis something nothing;
'Twas mine, tis his and has been slave to thousands:
But he that filches from me my good name
Robs me of that which not enriches him
And makes me poor indeed.
Othello:

If music be the food of love, play on.
Duke: **If music be the food of love, play on;**
Give me excess of it, that, surfeiting,
The appetite may sicken, and so die.
That strain again; it had a dying fall:
O, it came over my ear like the sweet sound,
That breathes upon a bank of violets,
Stealing and giving odor. Enough; no more.
Twelfth Night.

In a better world than this.
Le Beau: … But I can tell you that of late this duke
Hath taken displeasure against his gentle niece,
Grounded upon no other argument
But that the people praise her for her virtues
And pity her for her good father's sake;
And, on my life, his malice against the lady
Will suddenly break forth. Sir, fare you well:
Hereafter, **in a better world than this,**
I shall desire more love and knowledge of you.
As You Like It.

Sweet are the uses of adversity.
Duke Senior: Now, my co-mates and brothers in exile,
 Hath not old custom made this life more sweet
Than that of painted pomp? Are not these woods
More free from peril than the envious court?
Here feel we but the penalty of Adam,
The seasons' difference, as the icy fang
And churlish chiding of the winter's wind,
Which, when it bites and blows upon my body,
Even till I shrink with cold, I smile and say
'This is no flattery: these are counselors
That feelingly persuade me what I am.'
Sweet are the uses of adversity.
Which, like the toad, ugly and venomous,
Wears yet a precious jewel in his head.
As You Like It.

Good wine needs no bush.
Rosalind:
It is not the fashion to see the lady the epilogue;
But it is no more unhandsome than to see
The lord the prologue. If it be true that
Good wine needs no bush, 'tis true that a good play
Needs no epilogue; yet to good wine they do use good bushes,
And good plays prove the better by the help of good epilogues.
As You Like It.

The be-all and the end-all.
Poisoned chalice.
Even-handed justice.
Macbeth: If it were done when 'tis done, then 'twere well
It were done quickly: if the assassination
Could trammel up the consequence, and catch
With his surcease success; that but this blow
Might be **the be- all and the end-all** here,
But here, upon this bank and shoal of time,
We'ld jump the life to come. But in these cases
We still have judgment here; that we but teach
Bloody instructions, which, being taught, return
To plague the inventor: this **even-handed justice**
Commends the ingredients of our **poisoned chalice**
To our own lips…
Macbeth.

What's done is done.
Lady Macbeth: Naught's had all's spent.
Where our desire is got without content:
It's safer to be that which we destroy
Than by destruction dwell in doubtful joy.
How now, my lord; why do keep alone,
Of sorriest fancies your companions making,
Using those thoughts which should indeed have died
With them they think on? Things without all remedy
Should be without regard: **what's done is done.**
Macbeth: We have scotched the snake, not killed it.
Macbeth.

Cabined, Cribbed, Confined.
Macbeth: Then comes my fit again: I had else been perfect,
Whole as the marble, founded as the rock,
As broad and general as the casing air:
But now I am **cabined, cribbed, confined,**
Bound in to saucy doubts and fears.
Macbeth.

All our yesterdays.
Full of sound and fury.
Seyton: The queen, my lord is dead.
Macbeth: She should have died hereafter;
There would have been a time for such a word.
To-morrow, and to-morrow, and to-morrow,
Creeps in this petty pace from day to day
To the last syllable of recorded time,
And **all our yesterdays** have lighted fools
The way to dusty death. Out, out, brief candle;
Life's but a walking shadow, a poor player
That struts and frets his hour upon the stage
And then is heard no more: It is a tale
Told by an idiot, **full of sound and fury**
Signifying nothing.
 Macbeth.

Frailty, thy name is woman.
.. Heaven and earth.
Must I remember? Why, she would hang on him,
As if increase of appetite had grown
By what it fed on: and yet, within a month –
Let me not think on it – **Frailty, thy name is woman.**
Hamlet.

Neither a borrower nor a lender be.
To thine own self be true.
Polonius: **Neither a borrower nor a lender be;**
For loan oft loses both itself and friend,
And borrowing dulls the edge of husbandry.
This above all: **to thine own self be true,**
And it must follow, as the night the day,
Thou canst not then be false to any man.
Hamlet.

The primrose path.
Ophelia: I shall the effect of this good lesson keep
As watchman to my heart. But, good my brother,
Do not, as some ungracious pastors do,
Show me the steep and thorny way to heaven;
Whilst, like a puffed and reckless libertine,
Himself the **primrose path** of dalliance treads,
And recks not his own rede.
Hamlet:

One may smile and smile, and be a villain.
Hamlet: O most pernicious woman;
O villain, villain, smiling damned villain;
My tables, - meet it is I set it down,
That one may **smile, and smile, and be a villain.**
Hamlet.

Words, words, words.
Though this be madness, yet there is method in it.
Polonius: What do you read, my lord?
Hamlet: **Words, words, words.**
Polonius: What is the matter, my lord?
Hamlet: Between who?
Polonius: I mean, the matter that you read, my lord.
Hamlet: Slanders, sir: for the satirical rogue says
Here that old men have grey beards,
That their faces are wrinkled, their eyes
Purging thick amber and plum – tree gum
And that they have a plentiful lack of wit,
Together with most weak hams:
All which, sir, though I most powerfully and potently
Believe, yet I hold it not honesty to have it thus set down,
For yourself, sir, should be old as I am,
If like a crab you could go backward.
Polonius: (aside) **though this be madness, yet there is method in it.**
Hamlet.

Tell old tales, and laugh.
Who loses and who wins.
Who's in, who's out
The ebb and flow by the moon.
Cordelia: We are not the first
Who, with best meaning, have incurred the worst.
For thee, oppressed king, am I cast down;
Myself could else out-frown false fortune's frown.
Shall we not see these daughters and these sisters?
Lear: No no, no, no. Come, let's away to prison:
We two alone will sing like birds in the cage:
When thou dost ask me blessing, I'll kneel down,
And ask of thee forgiveness: so we'll live,
And pray, and sing, and **tell old tales, and laugh**
At gilded butterflies, and hear poor rogues
Talk of court news; and we'll talk with them too,
Who loses and who wins; who's in, who's out;
And take upon the mystery of things,
As if we were God's spies: and we'll wear out,
In a walled prison, packs and sects of great ones,
The ebb and flow by the moon.
King Lear.

Virgin-knot.
Prospero: Then, as my gift and thine own acquisition
Worthily purchased, take my daughter:
But if thou dost break her **virgin-knot** before
All sanctimonious ceremonies may
With full and holy rite be ministered
No sweet aspersion shall the heavens let fall
To make this contract grow; but barren hate,
Sour-eyed disdain and discord shall bestrew
The union of your bed with weeds so loathly
That you shall hate it both: therefore take heed,
As Hymen's lamps shall light you.
The Tempest.

The Quintessential Shakespeare

For his bounty,
there was no winter in it, an autumn it was,
that grew the more by reaping.

Antony and Cleopatra.

If it be true that good wine needs no bush,
Its true that a good play needs no epilogue,
Yet to good wine they do use good bushes,
And good plays prove the better by the help
 Of good epilogues.

As You Like It.

So we grew together,
Like to a double cherry; seeming parted,
But yet a union in partition,
Two lovely berries molded on one stem;
So, with two seeming bodies, but one heart.

A Midsummer Night's Dream.

O, be some other name.
What's in a name? That which we call a rose
by any other name would smell as sweet.

Romeo and Juliet.

So tedious is this day
as is the night before some festival
to an impatient child that hath new robes
and may not wear them.

Romeo and Juliet.

A woman moved is like a fountain troubled,
Muddy, ill-seeming, thick, bereft of beauty,
And while it is so, none so dry or thirsty

Will deign to sip or touch one drop of it.

The Taming of the Shrew.

All the world's a stage,
and all the men and women merely players.
They have their exits and their entrances.
And one man in his time plays many parts....

As You Like it.

To die, to sleep;
To sleep: perchance to dream: ay there's the rub;
For in that sleep of death what dreams may come
When we have shuffled off this mortal coil,
Must give us pause:

Hamlet.

But that the dread of something after death,
The undiscovered country from whose bourn
No traveller returns, puzzles the will
And makes us rather bear those ills we have
Than fly to others that we know not of?
Thus conscience does make cowards of us all.

Hamlet

But man, proud man;
Drest in a little brief authority,
Most ignorant of what he's most assured,
His glassy essence, like an angry ape,
Plays such fantastic tricks before high heaven
As make the angels weep; who, with our spleens,
Would all themselves laugh mortal.

Measure for Measure

Therefore to be possessed with double pomp,
To gild refined gold, to paint the lily,

To throw a perfume on the violet,
To smooth the ice, or add another hue
Unto the rainbow, or with taper-light
To seek the beauteous eye of heaven to garnish,
Is wasteful and ridiculous excess.

King John.

Give me my Romeo; and, when he shall die,
Take him and cut him out in little stars,
And he will make the face of heaven so fine
That all the world will be in love with night,
And pay no worship to the garish sun.

Romeo and Juliet.

The man that hath no muse in himself
nor is not moved with concord of sweet sounds,
Is fit for treasons, stratagems and spoils;
The motions of his spirit are dull as night
And his affections dark as Erebus:
Let no such man be trusted.

The Merchant of Venice.

For it's the mind that makes the body rich,
and as the sun breaks through the darkest clouds,
So honor peereth in the meanest habit.

The Taming of the Shrew.

Glory is like a circle in the water,
Which never ceaseth to enlarge itself,
Till by broad spreading it disperse to nought.

Henry V1 Part 1.

My bounty is as boundless as the sea.
My love as deep, the more I give to thee;
The more I have, for both are infinite.

Romeo and Juliet.

Good night, good night: Parting is such sweet sorrow;
That I shall say good night till it be morrow.

Romeo and Juliet.

I know him as myself, for from our infancy
We have conversed and spent our hours together:
And though myself have been an idle truant,
Omitting the sweet benefit of time
To clothe mine age with angle-like perfection…
Made use and fair advantage of his days;
His years but young but his experience of old;
His head unmellowed, but his judgment ripe;
And, in a word, for far behind his worth
Comes all the praises that I now bestow,
He is complete in feature and in mind
With all good grace to grace a gentleman.

The Two Gentlemen of Verona.

The heavens forbid
But that our loves and comforts should increase,
Even as our days do grow.

Othello.

Who steals my purse steals trash,
It's something, nothing; it was mine, it's his,
And has been slave to thousands:
But he that filches from me my good name
Robs me of that which not enriches him
and makes me poor indeed.

Othello.

It's not a year or two shows us a man:
They are all but stomachs, and we all but food;
They eat us hungrily, and when they are full,
They belch us.

Othello.

When I have plucked the rose,
I cannot give it vital growth again,
It must needs wither: I'll smell it on the tree.

Othello.

Between the acting of a dreadful thing
And the first motion, all the interim is
Like a phantasma, or a hideous dream.
The Genius and the mortal instruments
Are then in council; and the state of man,
Like to a little kingdom, suffers then
the nature of an insurrection.

Julius Caesar.

The heavens forbid
But that our loves and comforts should increase,
Even as our days do grow.

Othello.

Then comes my fit again: I had else been perfect,
Whole as the marble, founded as the rock,
As broad and general as the casing air:
But now I am cabined, cribbed, confined, bound in
To saucy doubts and fears.

Macbeth.

Wither should I fly?
I have done no harm. But I remember now
I am in this earthly world; where to do harm
is often laudable, to do good sometime
Accounted dangerous folly: why then, alas,
Do I put up that womanly defence,
To say I have done no harm?

Macbeth.

Cans't thou not minister to a mind diseased,
Pluck from the memory a rooted sorrow,
Raze out the written troubles of the brain,
And with some sweet oblivious antidote
Cleanse the stuffed bosom of that perilous stuff,
Which weighs upon the heart?

Macbeth.

She should have died hereafter;
There would have been a time for such a word.
To-morrow, and to-morrow, and to-morrow,
Creeps in this petty pace from day to day
To the last syllable of recorded time;
And all our yesterdays have lighted fools
The way to dusty death. Out, out, brief candle;
Life's but a walking shadow, a poor player
That struts and frets his hour upon the stage
And then is heard no more: it is a tale
Told by an idiot, full of sound and fury,
Signifying nothing.

Macbeth.

Brabantio:
Come, hither, gentle mistress:
Do you perceive in all this noble company
Where most you owe obedience?
Desdemona:
My noble father,
I do perceive here a divided duty:
To you I am bound for life and education;
My life and education both do learn me
How to respect you; you are the lord of duty;
I am hitherto your daughter: but here's my husband,
And so much duty as my mother showed

To you, preferring you before her father,
So much I challenge that I may profess
Due to the Moor my lord.

Othello.

When remedies are past, the griefs are ended
By seeing the worst, which late on hopes depended.
To mourn a mischief that is past and gone
is the next way to draw new mischief on.
What cannot be preserved when fortune takes
Patience her injury a mockery makes.
The robbed that smiles steals something from the thief;
He robs himself that spends a bootless grief.

Othello.

And these few precepts in thy memory
See thou character. Give thy thoughts no tongue,
Nor any unproportioned thought his act.
Be thou familiar, but by no means vulgar.
Those friends thou hast, and their adoption tried,
Grapple them to thy soul with hoops of steel;
But do not dull thy palm with entertainment
Of each new-hatched, unfledged comrade.
Beware of entrance to a quarrel; but being in,
Bear it that the opposed may beware of thee.
Give every man thy ear, but few thy voice.

Hamlet.

Neither a borrower nor a lender be;
For loan oft loses both itself and friend,
And borrowing dulls the edge of husbandry.
This above all: to thine own self be true,
And it must follow, as the night the day,
Thou canst not then be false to any man.

Hamlet.

Age cannot wither her, nor custom stale
Her infinite variety: other women cloy
the appetites they feed: but she makes hungry
Where most she satisfies: for vilest things
Become themselves in her; that the holy priests
Bless her when she is riggish.

Antony and Cleopatra.

Brutus:
You have done that you should be sorry for.
There is no terror, Cassius, in your threats,
For I am armed so strong in honesty
that they pass by me as the idle wind
which I respect not. I did send to you
For certain sums of gold, which you denied me:
For I can raise no money by vile means:
By heaven, I had rather coin my heart,
and drop my blood for drachmas, than to wring
from the hard hands of peasants their vile trash
by any indirection: I did send to you for gold
to pay my legions, which you denied me:
Was that done like Cassius? Should I have
answered Caius Cassius so? When Marcus Brutus
grows so covetous, to lock such rascal counters
from his friends, be ready, gods, with all your thunderbolts;
Dash him to pieces.

Julius Caesar.

When forty winters shall besiege thy brow,
And dig deep trenches in thy beauty's field,
Thy youth's proud livery, so gazed on now,
Will be a tattered weed, of small worth held:
Then being asked where all thy beauty lies,
Where all the treasure of thy lusty days,
To say, within thine own deep-sunken eyes,

Were an all-eating shame and thriftless praise.
How much more praise deserved thy beauty's use,
If thou couldst answer, 'This fair child of mine
Shall sum my count and make my old excuse,'
Proving his beauty by succession thine.
This were to be new made when thou art old,
And see thy blood warm when thou feel'st it cold.

Sonnet.11.

...Thou art thy mother's glass, and she in thee
Calls back the lovely April of her prime;
So thou through windows of thine age shall see
Despite of wrinkles this thy golden time.
But if thou live, remembered not to be,
Die single, and thine image dies with thee.

Sonnet 111.

...Then how, when nature calls thee to be gone,
What acceptable audit cans't thou leave?
Thy unused beauty must be tomb'd with thee,
Which, used, lives the executor to be.

Sonnet 1V

Music to hear, why hear'st thou music sadly?
Sweets with sweets war not, joy delights in joy....
Mark how one string, sweet husband to another,
Strikes each in each by mutual ordering,
Resembling sire and child and happy mother
Who all in one, one pleasing note do sing:
Whose speechless song, being many, seeming one,
Sings this to thee: 'Thou single wilt prove none.'

Sonnet V111.

Is it for fear to wet a widow's eye
that thou consumest thyself in single life?

Ah. If thou issueless shalt hap to die,
The world will wail thee, like a makeless wife
The world will be thy widow and still weep
That thou no form of thee hast left behind,
When every private widow well may keep
By children's eyes her husband's shape in mind.

Sonnet 1X.

When I do count the clock that tells the time,
And see the brave day sunk in hideous night;
When I behold the violet past prime,
And sable curls all silvered over with white;
When lofty trees I see barren of leaves
Which erst from heat did canopy the herd,
And summer's green all girded up in sheaves,
Borne on the bier with white and bristly beard,
Then of thy beauty do I question make,
That thou among the wastes of time must go,
Since sweets and beauties do themselves forsake
And die as fast as they see others grow;
And nothing against Time's scythe can make defence
Save breed, to brave him when he takes thee hence.

Sonnet X11

…So should that beauty which you hold in lease
Find no determination; then you were
yourself again after yourself's decease,
When your sweet issue your sweet form should bear,
Who lets so fair a house fall to decay,
Which husbandry in honor might uphold
Against the stormy gusts of winter's day
And barren rage of death's eternal cold?
O, none but unthrifts; Dear my love, you know
You had a father: Let your son say so.

Sonnet X111.

...But from thine eyes my knowledge I derive,
And, constant stars, in them I read such art
As truth and beauty shall together thrive,
If from thyself to store thou wouldst convert;
Or else of thee this I prognosticate:
Thy end is truth's and beauty's doom and date.

Sonnet X1V.

...If I could write the beauty of your eyes
And in fresh numbers number all your graces,
The age to come would say, ' This poet lies';
Such heavenly touches never touched earthly faces.

Sonnet XV11.

....
Shall I compare thee to a summer's day?
Thou art more lovely and more temperate:
Rough winds do shake the darling buds of May,
And summer's lease hath all too short a date:....

Sonnet XV111.

No more be grieved at that which thou hast done:
Roses have thorns, and silver fountains mud;
Clouds and eclipses stain both moon and sun,
And loathsome canker lives in sweetest bud.
All men make faults, and even I in this,
Authorizing thy trespass with compare,
Myself corrupting, salving thy amiss,
Excusing thy sins more than thy sins are;
For to thy sensual fault I bring in sense –
Thy adverse party is thy advocate –
And against myself a lawful plea commence:
Such civil was in my love and hate
That I an accessary needs must be
To that sweet thief which sourly robs from me.

Sonnet XXXV

As a decrepit father takes delight
To see his active child do deeds of youth,
So I, made lame by fortune's dearest spite,
Take all my comfort of thy world and truth.
For whether beauty, birth, or wealth, or wit,
Or any of these all, or all or more
Entitled in thy parts do crowned sit,
I make my love engrafted to this store:
So then I am not lame, poor, nor despised,
Whilst that this shadow doth such substance give
That I in my abundance am sufficed
And by a part of all thy glory live.
Look, what is best, that best I wish in thee:
This wish I have; then ten times happy me.

Sonnet XXXV11.

Not marble nor the gilded monuments
Of princes shall outlive this powerful rhyme.
...
When wasteful war shall statues overturn,
And broils root out the work of masonry,
Nor Mars his sword nor war's quick fire shall burn
The living record of your memory....

Sonnet LV

No longer mourn for me when I am dead
Than you shall hear the surly bell
Give warning to the world that I am fled
From this vile world, with vilest worms to dwell:
Nay, if you read this line, remember not
The hand that writ it; for I love you so
That I in your sweet thoughts would be forgot
If thinking on me then should make you woe.
O, if, I say, you look upon this verse
When I perhaps compounded am with clay,

Do not so much as my poor name rehearse,
But let your love even with my life decay,
Lest the wise world should look into your moan
And mock you with me after I am gone.

Sonnet LXX1.

That time of year thou mayst in me behold
when yellow leaves, or none, or few, do hang
upon those boughs which shake against the cold,
Bare ruined choirs, where late the sweet birds sang....

Sonnet LXX111

Let me not to the marriage of true minds
Admit impediments. Love is not love
Which alters when it alteration finds,
Or bends with the remover to remove:
O no, it is an ever-fixed mark
That looks on tempests and is never shaken;
It is the star to every wandering bark,
Whose worth's unknown, although his height be taken.
Love's not Time's Fool, though rosy lips and cheeks
Within his bending sickle's compass come;
Love alters not with his brief hours and weeks,
But bears it out even to the edge of doom.
If this be error and upon me proved,
I never writ, nor no man ever loved.

Sonnet CXV1

...Mad in pursuit and in possession so;
Had, having, and in quest to have, extreme;
A bliss in proof, and proved, a very woe;
Before, a joy proposed: behind a dream.
All this the world well knows; yet none knows well
to shun the heaven that leads men to this hell.

Sonnet CXX1X

King Richard 11.

...The name of King? O' God's name, let it go.
I'll give my jewels for a set of beads,
My gorgeous palace for a hermitage,
My gay apparel for an almsman's gown,
My figured goblets for a dish of wood,
My scepter for a palmer's walking-staff,
My subjects for a pair of carved saints,
And my large kingdom for a little grave,
A little little grave, an obscure grave;
Or I'll be buried in the King's highway,
Some way of common trade, where subjects' feet
May hourly trample on their sovereign's head;
For on my heart they tread now whilst I live;
And buried once, why not upon my head? ... .
 Bolingbroke:
...I thought you had seen willing to resign.

King Richard 11:

My crown I am; but still my griefs are mine.
You may my glories and my state depose,
but not my griefs; still I am king of those.

Richard 11

If music be the food of love, play on,
Give me excess of it, that, surfeiting,
The appetite may sicken, and so die.
That strain again. It had a dying fall.

Twelfth Night.

No matter where; of comfort no man speak:
Let's talk of graves, of worms and epitaphs;
Make dust our paper, and with rainy eyes
write sorrow on the bosom of the earth.

Let's choose executors and talk of wills:
And yet not so; for what can we bequeath
Save our deposed bodies to the ground?

Richard 11.

...For God's sake let us sit upon the ground
And tell sad stories of the death of kings;
How some have been deposed, some slain in war,
Some haunted by the ghosts they have deposed,
Some poisoned by their wives, some sleeping killed,
All murdered: for within the hollow crown
That rounds the mortal temples of a king
Keeps Death his court and there the music sits,
Scoffing his state and grinning at his pomp....

Richard 11.

...Why, I can smile, and murder whiles I smile,
And cry 'Content' to that which grieves my heart,
And wet my cheeks with artificial tears,
And frame my face to all occasions.

Henry V1.

What a piece of work is a man;
How noble in reason;
How infinite in faculty;
In form and moving,
How express and admirable;
In action how like an angel;
In apprehension how like a god;
The beauty of the world,
The paragon of animals.
And yet, to me, what is this quintessence of dust?
Man delights not me: no, nor woman neither
Though by your smiling you seem to say so.

Hamlet

See how she leans her cheek upon her hand;
O, that I were a glove upon that hand,
That I might touch that cheek.

Romeo and Juliet.

I pray you, think you question with the Jew:
You may as well go stand upon the beach
And bid the main flood bate his usual height;
You may as well use question with the wolf
Why he hath made the ewe bleat for the lamb;
You may as well forbid the mountain pines
To wag their high tops and to make no noise,
When they are fretten with the gusts of heaven;
You may as well do anything most hard,
As seek to soften that —than which what's harder?
His Jewish heart: therefore, I do beseech you,
Make no more offers, use no farther means,
But with all brief and plain conveniency
Let me have judgment and the Jew his will.

The Merchant of Venice.

I, that am rudely stamped, and want love's majesty
To strut before a wanton ambling nymph;
I, that am curtailed of this fair proportion,
Cheated of feature by dissembling nature,
Deformed, unfinished, sent before my time
Into this breathing world, scarce half made up,
And that so lamely and unfashionable
That dogs bark at me as I halt by them;

Richard 111.

Nurse: Madam:
Juliet: Nurse.
Nurse: Your lady mother is coming to your chamber:
The day is broke; be wary, look about.
Juliet: Then, window, let day in, and let life out.

Romeo: Farewell, farewell, one kiss, and I'll descend.
Juliet: Art thou gone so? Love, lord, ay, husband, friend;
I must hear from thee every day in the hour,
For in a minute there are many days:
O, by this count I shall be much in years
Ere I again behold my Romeo.
Romeo: Farewell. I will omit no opportunity
That may convey my greetings, love to thee.
Juliet: O, think'st thou we shall ever meet again?
Romeo: I doubt it not; and all these woes shall serve
For sweet discourses in our time to come.
Juliet: O God, I have an ill-divining soul;
Methinks I see thee, now thou art below,
As one dead in the bottom of a tomb:
Either my eyesight fails, or thou look'st pale.
Romeo: And trust me, love, in my eye so do you:
Dry sorrow drinks our blood. Adieu, adieu.
Juliet: O fortune, fortune. All men call thee fickle:
If thou art fickle, what dost thou with him
That is renown's for faith? Be fickle, fortune;
For then, I hope, thou wilt not keep him long,
But send him back.

Romeo and Juliet.

SHORT BITES FROM
SHAKESPEARE

Who so firm that cannot be seduced.

Julius Caesar.

God made him, and therefore let him pass for a man.

The Merchant of Venice.

The smallest worm will turn being trodden on.

Henry V1.

The hind that would be mated by the lion must die for love.

All's Well That Ends Well.

Patience is sottish, and impatience does become a dog that's mad.

Antony and Cleopatra.

The stroke of death is as a lover's pinch, which hurts, and is desired.

Antony and Cleopatra.

Falsehood is worse in kings than beggars.

Cymbeline.

Plenty and peace breeds cowards.

Cymbeline.

The fault, dear Brutus, is not in our stars
But in ourselves, that we are underlings.

Julius Caesar.

When beggars die, there are no comets seen;
The heavens themselves blaze forth the death of princes.

Julius Caesar.

Love looks not with the eyes, but with the mind;
And therefore is winged Cupid painted blind.

A Midsummer Night's Dream.

Too little payment for so great a debt.

The Taming Of the Shrew.

Men prize the thing ungained more than it is.

Troilus and Cressida.

My thoughts were like unbridled children, grown too
Headstrong for their mother.

Troilus and Cressida.

O time, thou untangle this, not I; It is too hard a knot for me to
untie.

Twelfth Night.

If music be the food of love, play on.

Twelfth Night.

Golden lads and girls all must, as chimney-sweepers, come to dust.

Cymbeline.

Society is no comfort to one not sociable.

Cymbeline.

What is a man, if his chief good and market of his time
Be but to sleep and feed? A beast no more.

Hamlet.

Ingratitude, thou marble-hearted fiend, more hideous when thou
Showest thee in a child, than the sea-monster.

King Lear.

When he is best, he is a little worse than a man,
And when he is worst, he is a little better than a beast.

The Merchant of Venice.

Small things make base men proud.

Henry V1.

Unbidden guests are often welcomest when they are gone.

Henry V1.

Talkers are no good doers.

Richard 111.

Small cheer and great welcome makes a merry feast.

The Comedy of Errors.

Ill deeds are doubled with an evil word.

The Comedy of Errors.

There is small choice in rotten apples.

The Taming of the Shrew.

How poor are they that have not patience;
What wound did ever heal but by degrees.

Othello.

Yet fruits that blossom first will first be ripe.

Othello.

As flies to wanton boys, are we to the gods, they kill us for their sport.

King Lear.

What, wouldst thou have a serpent sting thee twice?

The Merchant of Venice.

The weakest kind of fruit drops earliest to the ground.

The Merchant of Venice.

So young a body with so old a head.

The Merchant of Venice.

A little pot and soon hot.

The Taming of the Shrew.

A woman moved is like a fountain troubled,
Muddy, ill-seeming, thick, bereft of beauty.

The Taming of the Shrew.

A heavy heart bears not a nimble tongue.

Love's Labor's Lost.

The words of Mercury are harsh after the songs of Apollo.

Love's Labor's Lost.

Dreams which are the children of an idle brain.

Romeo and Juliet.

The devil can cite Scripture for his purpose.

The Merchant of Venice.

For sufferance is the badge of all our tribe.

The Merchant of Venice.

He jests at scars that never felt a wound.

Romeo and Juliet.

What's in a name? That which we call a rose
By any other name would smell as sweet.

Romeo and Juliet.

Good night, good night, parting is such sweet sorrow.

Romeo and Juliet.

In a minute there are many days.

Romeo and Juliet.

Cowards die many times before their deaths;
The valiant never taste of death but once.

Julius Caesar

There is a tide in the affairs of men,
Which, taken at the flood, leads to fortune.

Julius Caesar.

It's safer to be that which we destroy
Than by destruction dwell in doubtful joy.

Macbeth.

False face must hide what the false heart doth know.

Macbeth.

That one may smile, and smile, and be a villain.

Hamlet.

There are more things in heaven and earth, Horatio
Than are dreamt of in your philosophy.

Hamlet.

Brevity is the soul of wit.

Hamlet.

An old man is twice a child.

Hamlet.

Thus conscience does make cowards of us all.

Hamlet.

Suit the action to the word.

Hamlet.

Our thoughts are ours, their ends none of our own.

Hamlet.

Be soft as sinews of the new-born babe.

Hamlet.

My words fly up, my thoughts remain below.

Hamlet.

When sorrows come, they come not single spies, but in battalions.

Hamlet.

The cat will mew and dog will have his day.

Hamlet.

I must be cruel, only to be kind.

Hamlet.

Good night, sweet prince; and flights of angels sing thee to thy rest.

Hamlet

How sharper than a serpent's tooth it is to have a thankless child.

King Lear.

We cannot all be masters, nor all masters cannot be truly followed.

Othello.

Who steals my purse steals trash….But he that filches from me my good name
Robs me of that which not enriches him and makes me poor indeed.

Othello.

Life is as tedious as a twice-told tale.

King John.

My salad days, when I was green in judgment.

Antony and Cleopatra.

Celerity (rapidity of motion) is never more admired than by the negligent.

Antony and Cleopatra.

The robbed that smiles steals something from the thief;
He robs himself that spends a bootless grief.

Othello.

We lose it not, so long as we can smile.

Othello.

When valor preys on reason, it eats the sword it fights with.

Antony and Cleopatra.

There is some soul of goodness in things evil,
Would men observingly distil it out.

King Henry V.

Where having nothing, nothing can he lose.

King Henry V1.

He is a dreamer, let us leave him; pass.

Julius Caesar.

Cry havoc and let slip the dogs of war.

Julius Caesar.

In time we hate that which we often fear.

Antony and Cleopatra.

But gold that's put to use more gold begets.

Venus and Adonis.

Love comforts like sunshine after rain,
But lust's effect is tempest after sun.

Venus and Adonis.

How love makes young men thrall and old men dote.

Venus and Adonis.

For lovers' hours are long, though seeming short.

Venus and Adonis.

Who buys a minute's mirth to wail a week?

The Rape of Lucrece.

For one sweet grape who will the vine destroy?

The Rape of Lucrece.

Men's faults do seldom to themselves appear;
Their own transgressions partially they smother.

The Rape of Lucrece.

Small lights are soon blown out, huge fires abide.

The Rape of Lucrece.

Who, having two sweet babes, when death takes one,
Will slay the other and be nurse to none.

The Rape of Lucrece.

Though men can cover crimes with bold stern looks,
Poor women's faces are their own faults' books.

The Rape of Lucrece.

For sorrow, like a heavy-hanging bell,
Once set on ringing, with his own weight goes.

The Rape of Lucrece.

Though woe be heavy, yet it seldom sleeps;
And they that watch see time how slow it creeps.

The Rape of Lucrece.

The old bees die, the young possess their hive.

The Rape of Lucrece.

But if thou live, remembered not to be,
Die single, and thine image dies with thee.

Sonnet. 111.

When I consider everything that grows,
Holds in perfection but a little moment…

Sonnet XV

But if the while I think on thee, dear friend,
All losses are restored and sorrows end.

Sonnet. XXX

Like as the waves make towards the pebbled shore,
So do our minutes hasten to their end.

Sonnet. LX

For sweetest things turn sourest by their deeds;
Lilies that fester smell far worse than weeds.

Sonnet. XC1V.

And loathsome canker lives in sweetest bud.

Sonnet. XXXV.

Our remedies oft in ourselves do lie;
Which we ascribe to heaven.

All's Well That Ends Well.

Why, what is pomp, rule, reign, but earth and dust?
And, live we how we can, yet die we must.

Henry V1.

Present fears are less than horrible imaginings.

Macbeth.

Who alone suffers, suffers most in the mind.

King Lear.

O, how wretched
Is that poor man that hangs on Princes' favors.

Henry V111.

I wasted time, and now doth time waste me.

Richard 11.

If all the year were playing holidays,
To sport would be as tedious as to work.

Henry 1V.

What infinite heart's ease must kings neglect
That private men enjoy.

Henry V.

My brain more busy than the laboring spider
Weaves tedious snares to trap mine enemies.

Henry V1.

O Tiger's heart wrapped in a woman's hide.

Henry V1 Part 111.

Good wombs have borne bad sons.

Tempest.

You rub the sore, when you should bring the plaster.

Tempest.

Misery acquaints a man with strange bed-fellows.

Tempest.

Travelers never did lie though fools at home condemn them.

Tempest.

A lover's eyes will gaze an eagle blind,
A lover's ear will hear the lowest sound.

Love's Labor's Lost.

Like little wanton boys that swim on bladders.

Henry V111.

Shakespeare, His women and I

Portia in Julius Caesar:

The conspirators have agreed that Caesar should be assassinated as in their opinion he has become too ambitious and therefore a threat to the Republic. Brutus is a disturbed man the night before the assassination. In the following dialogue we see Portia as a faithful wife intelligently arguing why Brutus's secret is safe with her. She presents her case so cleverly that Brutus is left without an answer.

Portia: Brutus, my lord.

Brutus: Portia, what mean you? Wherefore rise you now? It is not for your health thus to commit your weak condition to the raw cold morning.

Portia: Nor for yours neither. You have ungently Brutus, stole from my bed, and yesternight, at supper, you suddenly arose, and walked about, musing, and sighing, with your arms across; and when I asked you what the matter was, you stared upon me with ungentle looks.

I urged you further: then you scratched your head, and too impatiently stamped with your foot; **yet I insisted,** yet you answered not, but, with an angry wafture of your hand gave sign for me to leave you. So I did; fearing to strengthen that impatience which seemed too much enkindled, and withal hoping it was but an effect of humor, which sometime hath **his hour with every man**. (Portia treads very softly here)

It will not let you eat, nor talk, nor sleep; and could it work so much upon your shape as it has much prevailed on your condition, I should not know you, Brutus. Dear my lord. **Make me acquainted with your cause of grief.**

Brutus dismisses it casually.

Brutus: I am not well in health, and that is all.

Portia intelligently counters.

Portia: Brutus is wise, and, were he not in health, he would embrace the means to come by it.

Brutus is again dismissive.

Brutus: Why so I do. Good Portia, go to bed.

Portia insists and with clarity and civility presents further her case.

Portia: Is Brutus sick? And is it physical to walk unbraced and suck up the humors of the dank morning? What, is Brutus sick, and will he steal out of his wholesome bed, to dare the vile contagion of the night and tempt the rheumy and unpurged air to add unto his sickness? No, my Brutus; you have some sick offence within your mind, (Now Portia makes a stronger case)

Which, by the right and virtue of my place, I ought to know of: and, upon my knees, I charm you, by my once- commended beauty, by all your vows of love, and that great vow which did incorporate and make us one. That you unfold to me, yourself, your half, why you are heavy, and what men to-night have had resort to you…

Brutus: Kneel not, gentle Portia.

Portia makes a yet stronger case turning his words against him…

Portia**: I should not need, if you were gentle Brutus.** Within the bond of marriage, tell me, Brutus, is it excepted, I should know no secrets that appertain to you? Am I yourself but, as it were, in sort or limitation, to keep with you at meals, comfort your bed, and talk to you sometimes? Dwell I but in the suburbs of your good pleasure? If it be no more, **Portia is Brutus' harlot, not his wife.**

Brutus hopes he could get by.

Brutus: You are my true and honorable wife. As dear to me as are the ruddy drops that visit my sad heart.

Portia does not give up. She presents her excellent credentials:

Portia: If this were true, then should I know this secret. **I grant I am a woman**, (this is just a ploy) **but withal a woman that Lord Brutus took to wife: I grant I am a woman; but withal a woman well- reputed, Cato's daughter. Think you I am no stronger than my sex, being so fathered, and so husbanded?** (How could one ignore this compliment?)

"Tell me your counsels, I will not disclose them." (Portia cuts herself in the thigh and suffers the pain in silence to prove she is stronger than her sex) **"I have made strong proof of my constancy, giving myself a voluntary wound here, in the thigh: can I bear that with patience, and not my husband's secrets?"**

Brutus: O ye gods, render me worthy of this noble wife.

In the end, Brutus promises to tell her what has been troubling him.

Lady Macbeth in Macbeth

We witness in "Macbeth" the manipulative, ambitious, scheming, strong- willed woman – Lady Macbeth as contrasted with a hesitant, reflective husband.

Macbeth and wife want the throne of Scotland. The way to achieve this is to kill the king on his visit. Lady Macbeth is aware that her husband has to be egged on, even taunted to act. "Yet do I fear thy nature; it is too full of the milk of human kindness"

She hears King Duncan is due and she prepares her mood for the murder. We see her vicious nature in full bloom. "Come, you spirits that tend on mortal thoughts, **unsex me here** (she wants the strength of a man) and fill me from the crown to the toe top-full of direst cruelty. Make thick my blood; Stop up the access and passage to remorse, that no compunctious visitings of nature shake my fell purpose, nor keep peace between the effect and it. Come to my woman's breasts and take my milk for gall"

Lady Macbeth instructs Macbeth how he should conduct himself. "Bear welcome in your eye, your hand, your tongue: **look like the innocent flower, but be the serpent under it…**"

Macbeth wavers. He says like all procrastinators, "We will speak further." Lady Macbeth says you just do it and "Leave the rest to me." At one point Macbeth gets cold feet and asks, "If we should fail?" and here is how Lady Macbeth responds. **"We fail. But screw your courage to the sticking – place, and we'll not fail."**

Lady Macbeth planned it all. King Duncan is murdered and disaster follows.

Ophelia in Hamlet.

Ophelia comes across as a weak-minded person. Neglected and insulted by Hamlet who to her was "the glass of fashion and the mold of form", "the observed of all observers", compounded further by the sadness over her father's death, she finally loses her mind.

Ophelia's brother Laertes in a long and wordy speech cautions the sister not to put too much faith in marrying Hamlet, the prince ("for on his choice depends the safety and health of this whole state") which would lead him away from her. He goes on:

"Then weigh what loss your honor may sustain…or lose your heart or your chaste treasure open to his unmastered importunity. Fear it, Ophelia, fear it, my dear sister, and keep you in the rear of your affection, out of the shot and danger of desire...." He cautions her to be wary. "Best safety lies in fear."

Ophelia even in a distressed state of mind gives this classic, memorable reply.

"I shall the effect of this good lesson keep as watchman to my heart. But, good my brother, do not, as some ungracious pastors do, show me the steep and thorny way to heaven ; whilests, like a puffed and reckless libertine, himself the primrose path of dalliance treads, and recks not his own rede." Laertes has no reply.

The sisters in King Lear.

In King Lear we see three sisters behave just the way human beings behave most of the time. Four hundred years ago or four hundred years from now, time will have no effect on human nature.
King Lear is of advanced age. He has decided to divide his kingdom among his three daughters. The daughters are: the eldest – Goneril, the second – Regan and the youngest, his favorite – Cordelia.

The King would like to know, "Tell me, my daughters, – since now we will divest us, both of rule, interest of territory, cares of state – which of you shall we say doth love us most?"

Goneril and Regan go to extremes in professing their love for the father.

Goneril: "Sir, I love you more than words can wield the matter. Dearer than eye-sight, space and liberty..."

Going second Regan does one better: "Sir, I am made of the self-same metal that my sister is, and prize me at her worth; in my true heart; I find she names my very deed of love; **only she comes too short:"**

The father now turns to his favorite, Cordelia. "Now our joy, although the last, not least... what can you say to draw a third more opulent than your sisters? Speak.

Cordelia: Nothing, my lord.

Lear: Nothing.

Cordelia: Nothing.

The father cautions. Nothing will come of nothing; speak again.

Cordelia does not waver even though Lear gives her another chance: "How, how, Cordelia. Mend your speech a little, lest it may mar your fortunes."

Cordelia explains truthfully:

"Good my lord, you have begot me, bred me, loved me: I return those duties back as are right fit, obey you, love you, and most honor you. Why have my sisters' husbands, if they say they love you all? **Haply, when I shall wed, that lord, whose hand must take my plight, shall carry half my love with him, half my care and duty: Sure, I shall never marry like my sisters, to love my father all."**

The father gives his favorite one more opportunity to retract. "But goes thy heart with this?

Cordelia: Ay, good my lord....

Lear: "**Better thou hadst not been born than not to have pleased me better."**

The arrangement with Cornelia and Regan was that the father will live one month with one daughter and then with the other accompanied by one hundred knights.

The two older sisters even though they professed much love treat the father with utter contempt. He is turned away from their homes bag and baggage. Goneril refers to the father: "Idle old man that still would manage those authorities that he hath given away. Now, by my life, old fools are babes again"

The father hoping the other daughter, Regan will be kind to him goes to her house. Here again the daughter is cruel. She would not have the father with his large entourage. He is driven out into the stormy night.

Lear is driven to utter: "I am a very foolish man, fond old man, fourscore and upward; not an hour more or less; and, to deal plainly, I fear I am not in my perfect mind. Methinks I should know you, and know this man; yet I am doubtful…" He then recognizes his daughter Cordelia, who is weeping seeing the condition the father is in. The father pleads, "Be your tears wet? Yes, faith. I pray weep not; if you have poison for me, I will drink it. I know you do not love me, for your sisters have, as I do remember, done me wrong: You have some cause, they have not.

Cordelia replies, "No cause, no cause."

They become close friends:

Lear: ".. we too alone will sing like birds in the cage: when thou dost ask me blessing, I'll kneel down and ask of thee forgiveness: so we'll live and pray, and sing, and tell old tales, and laugh at gilded butterflies, and hear poor rogues talk of court news; and we'll talk with them too; who loses and who wins; who's in, who's out; and take upon's the mystery of things, as if we were God's spies: and we'll wear out in a walled prison, packs and sects of great ones, that ebb and flow by the moon."

Portia in "The Merchant of Venice."

In my opinion in The Merchant of Venice we see the smartest woman among all of Shakespeare's women, Portia. Her newly wed husband's best friend Antonio is about to lose his life.

Portia's husband, Bassanio had borrowed money, three thousand ducats from, Shylock the Jew to pay for his travel to Belmont

K. B. Chandra Raj

where he successfully marries Portia. Bassanio's best friend Antonio guaranteed the loan. Failure to repay would result in Shylock having the right to cut a pound of flesh from Antonio's body.

Antonio's trading ships flounder in the high seas and he is unable to come up with the money on the appointed date and the pound of flesh is forfeit to Shylock who is determined to have it. Portia in disguise as a man unknown to Bassanio and Antonio appears in court as Attorney for Antonio. It's here that we see Shakespeare's Portia at her best. She first offers Shylock large sums of money and Shylock refuses it. He wants his pound of flesh. She then changes her tactic. She appeals to his better angels in the now popular "The quality of mercy" speech. Shylock is unmoved. He is determined to have his pound of flesh. Now Portia 'goes for the jugular'

She says to the utter delight of shylock that he may have his pound of flesh. "The law allows it, and the court awards it."

Portia: The Jew shall have all justice.. He shall have nothing but the penalty... Therefore prepare thee to cut off the flesh. Shed thou no blood, nor cut thou less nor more or less than a just pound, be it but so much as makes it light or heavy in the substance, or the division of the twentieth part of one poor scruple; nay if the scale do turn but in the estimation of a hair, thou diest and all thy goods are confiscate.

Shylock: Give me my principal, and let me go.

Katharina in "The Taming of the Shrew."

In this play we see Shakespeare's Katharina very ably having 'verbal fisticuffs' with her suitor, Petruchio. Even though this intrepid shrew is ultimately "tamed" it was not before she gave back as much as she got.

Powered by the twin engine of quick wit and humor they steam along with all cylinders firing. The exchanges between the two make entertaining reading.

Petruchio: Good morrow, Kate; for that's your name, I hear.

Katharina: Well have you heard, but something hard of hearing: They call me Katharina that do talk of me.

Petruchio: You lie, in faith; for you are called plain Kate and bonny Kate and sometimes Kate the curst; But Kate, the prettiest Kate in Christendom, Kate of Kate Hall, my super- dainty Kate…hearing thy mildness praised in every town, thy virtues spoke of, and thy beauty sounded, yet not so deeply as to thee belongs, myself am **moved** to woo thee for my wife.

Katharina: **Moved.** In good time let him that **moved** you hither **remove** you hence; I knew you at the first you were a **moveable.**

Petruchio: Why, what's a **moveable?**

Katharina: A joined stool.

Petruchio: Thou hast hit it; come, sit on me.

Katharina: Asses are made to bear, and so are you.

Petruchio: Women are made to bear, and so are you.

Katharina: No such jade as you, if me you mean.

Petruchio: Alas. Good Kate, I'll not burden thee; for, knowing thee to be but young and light –

Katharina: Too light for such a swain as you to catch and yet as heavy as my weight should be.

Prtruchio: Should be. Should –buzz.

Katharina: Well taken, and like a buzzard.

Petruchio: O slow-winged turtle. Shall a buzzard take thee?

Katharina: Ay, for a turtle, as he takes a buzzard.

Petruchio: Come, come, you wasp; in faith you are too angry.

Katharina: If I be waspish, best beware my sting.

Petruchio: My remedy is then, to pluck it out.

Katharina: Ay, if the fool could find it where it lies.

Petruchio: Who knows not where a wasp does wear his sting? In his tail.

Katharina: In his tongue.

Petruchio: Whose tongue?

Katharina: Yours, if you talk of tails: and so farewell.

Petruchio: What, with my tongue in your tail? Nay, come again, Good Kate; I am a gentleman.

Katharina: That I'll try. (She strikes him)
Petruchio: I swear I'll cuff you, if you strike again.
Katharina; So may you lose your arms: If you strike me, you are no gentleman; and if no gentleman, why then no arms.
Petruchio: A herald, Kate? O, put me in thy books.
Katharina: What is your crest? A coxcomb?
Petruchio: A combless cock, so Kate will be my hen.
Katharina: No cock of mine: you crow too like a craven.
Petruchio: Nay, come, Kate, come; you must not look so sour.
Katharina: It is my fashion, when I see a crab.
Petruchio: Why, here's no crab; and therefore look not sour.
Katharina: There is, there is.
Petruchio: Then show it me.
Katharina; Had I a glass, I would.
Petruchio: What, you mean my face?
Katharina: Well aimed of such a young one.
Petruchio: Now, by Saint George, I am too young for you.
Katharina: Yet you are withered.
Petruchio: It's with cares.
Katharina: I care not..
Katharina: Where did you study all this goodly speech?
Petruchio: It is extempore, from my mother-wit.
Katharina: A witty mother. Witless else her son.

Desdemona in Othello:

In this play as in the case of Cordelia in King Lear we see Desdemona rationally and intelligently explaining to her father why she would disobey him.

Desdemona, the only daughter of Brabantio has run away with a black man, Othello and this has saddened him greatly. The father thinks her daughter is a victim of witchcraft. Desdemona is summoned to stand before the council and has to now choose between her father and her husband.

Brabantio: Come hither, gentle mistress: Do you perceive in all this noble company, where must you owe obedience?

Desdemona replies with love, respect and sound reasoning:

My noble father, I do perceive here a divided duty: To you I am bound for life and education; My life and education both do learn me how to respect you; you are the lord of duty; I am hitherto your daughter: but here's my husband, and so much duty as my mother showed to you, preferring you before her father, so much I challenge that I may profess due to the Moor my lord.

Cleopatra in Antony and Cleopatra.

Cleopatra's is a Rubik's cube kind of personality; one of many dimensions and attributes, each full blown. The ultimate seductive woman; she is regal, passionate, sensuous, saucy and possessed of irresistible allure and beauty, cute and cunning. She was of Greek Macedonian descent, a "naturalized" Egyptian. She was the first woman to rule single handed without a male prop. A super hawk in the modern sense, she was an astute naval commander.

Hers' was an explosive personality with an arsenal of lethal weapons. She had the uncanny talent to be able to pick the appropriate weapon determined by the circumstances to bring down her prey.

Demonstrating inexorable hubris she could stand her ground if that was what was required. The mighty Mark Antony could not order her. " **Upon her landing, Antony sent to her, invited her to supper: she replied, it should be better he became her guest**; which she entreated: our courteous Antony, whom never the word of 'No' woman heard speak, being barbered ten times over, goes to the feast, and for his ordinary pays his heart for what his eyes eat only."

Cleopatra could be manipulative. When Antony shows signs that he will indeed answer the summons to Rome, she sends her serving woman, Charmaine to seek him out and "if you find him sad say I am dancing; if in mirth, report that I am sudden sick."

Her fierce temper was a tool in her hands. When an innocent messenger brings news of the marriage between Octavia and Antony, she flies into a rage. **"The most infectious pestilence upon thee (strikes him down) what say you? Hence, horrible villain, or I'll spurn thine eyes like balls before me, I'll unhair thy head; thou shalt be whipped with wire, and stewed in brine, smarting in lingering pickle."**

Cleopatra had her human side as well. Plagued by doubt, envy and insecurity, she is desperate to know from the messenger all about Octavia whom Marc Antony had married.

Cleopatra: Did thou behold Octavia?
Messenger: Ay, dread Queen.
Cleopatra: Where?
Messenger: Madam in Rome..
Cleopatra: Is she as tall as me?
Messenger: She is not, madam
Cleopatra: Didst hear her speak? Is she shrill- tongued or low?
Messenger: Madam, I heard her speak. She is low- voiced
Cleopatra: That's not so good. He cannot like her long…
Cleopatra: Guess at her years, I prithee.
Messenger: Madam, she was a widow.
Cleopatra: Widow. Charmian, hark.
Messenger: And I do think she is thirty.
Cleopatra: Bears't thou her face in mind? Is it long or round?
Messenger: Round even to faultness.
Cleopatra: For the most part, too, they are foolish that are so. Her hair, what color?
Messenger: Brown, Madam. And her forehead as low as she would wish it

When Antony is dying Cleopatra thinks only of her predicament.

Cleopatra: "**Noblest of men, woo't die? Has thou no care of me? Shall I abide in this dull world, which in thy absence is no better than a sty?**"

Cleopatra keeps her honor and pride intact. Rather than be paraded by Octavius Caesar as a whore she kills herself. She dies calmly and ecstatically, imagining how she will meet Antony again in the afterlife - what Hindu wives believed when they performed suttee.

Cleopatra: "Give me my robe, put on my crown: I have immortal longings in me: now no more the juice of Egypt's grape shall moist this lip: .. Methinks I hear Antony call; I see him rouse himself to praise my noble act."

Cleopatra was endowed with penetrating intelligence. She spoke nine languages fluently and was better at the tenth – flattery. Possessed of a mega - watt charisma, she used for the most part her biological blessings to divine her destiny. Her sexual prowess was so overpowering that her intellectual acuity was sometimes lost in it.

She manipulated her largely illiterate subjects with lavish shows of pomp and grandeur into believing in her divinity:

"The barge she sat in, like a burnished throne; Burned on the water: the poop was beaten gold; Purple the sails, and so perfumed that; the winds were love-sick with them; the oars were silver, which to the tune of flutes kept stroke, and made the water which they beat to follow faster, as amorous of their strokes. For her own person, it beggared all description."

When required she could be ruthless in the pursuit of her goal. She married her two brothers and killed them and arranged the murder of her sister. She was not disposed to sharing power.

Cleopatra who died at the age of thirty nine before Jesus was born remains to this day, "one of the busiest after lives in history. "An asteroid, a video game, a cigarette, a slot machine, a strip

club" and every year on Halloween night Cleopatra can be seen trick – or - treating.

Some where there surely must be a pizza named, "Cleopatra"

The power of Shakespeare's words

The goodness of Miranda in "The Tempest"

Miranda's plea to the father for the safety of those caught in the storm – persons totally unknown to her.

Miranda: "If by your art, my dearest father, you have put the wild waters in this roar, allay them. The sky, it seems, would pour down stinking pitch, but that the sea, mounting to the welkin's cheek, dashes the fire out. O, I have suffered with those that I saw suffer; a brave vessel, who had, no doubt, some noble creature in her, dashed all to pieces. O, the cry did knock against my very heart. Poor souls, they perished. **Had I been any god of power, I would have sunk the sea within the earth** or ere it should the good ship so have swallowed and the fraughting souls within her."

Miranda who was cast away in a lonely island has this to say about her life:

"O, wonder. How many goodly creatures are there here. How beauteous mankind is. O brave new world that has such people in it." We cannot help but fondly recall Anne Franke.

Shylock's hard hearted intransigence in "The Merchant of Venice"

Shylock is offered six thousand **ducats** for the three thousand owed to him and he replies.

"If every ducat in six thousand ducats were in six parts and every part a ducat, I would not draw them; **I would have my bond**"... which is the pound of flesh off Antonio's body.

To the question, "How shall thou hope for mercy, rendering none?" Here is his reply

"What judgment shall I dread, doing no wrong? You have among you many a purchased slave, which, like your asses and your dogs and your mules, you use in abject and in slavish parts, because you bought them: shall I say to you, let them be free, marry them to your heirs? Why sweat they under burthens? Let their beds be made as soft as yours and let their palates be seasoned with such viands? You will answer, "The slaves are ours": so do I answer you: **The pound of flesh, which I demand of him is dearly bought; its mine and I will have it.** If you deny me, fie upon your law. There is no force in the decrees of Venice. I stand for judgment: answer; shall I have it?

Juliet's unqualified love for Romeo in "Romeo and Juliet"

Juliet: "Art thou gone so? Love, lord, ay, husband, friend. I must hear from thee every day in the hour, for in a minute there are many days; O, by this count I shall be much in years ere I again behold my Romeo."

The introspective, tortured Hamlet in "Hamlet"

We witness here Hamlet doing with words what Silas the albino monk in Da Vinci code does with a metal cilice - flogging him

"To die: to sleep; no more; and by a sleep to say we end the heart-ache and the thousand natural shocks that flesh is heir to, it's a consummation devoutly to be wished. To die, to sleep; to sleep: perchance to dream: ay, there's the rub; **For in that sleep of death what dreams may come when we have shuffled off this mortal coil, must give us pause**:...to grunt and sweat under a weary life, **but that the dread of something after death, the undiscovered country from whose bourn no traveller returns, puzzles the will and makes us rather bear those ills we have than fly to others that we know not of?** Thus conscience does make cowards of us all."

The jealous Cassius conspiring to murder Caesar in "Julius Caesar"

Cassius: "Why, man, he doth bestride the narrow world like a Colossus, and we petty men walk under his huge legs and peep about to find ourselves dishonorable graves. Men at some time are masters of their fates: The fault, dear Brutus, is not in our stars, but in ourselves, that we are underlings. Brutus and Caesar: what should be in that 'Caesar'? Why should that name be sounded more than yours? Write them together, yours is as fair a name; sound them, it doth become the mouth as well; weigh them, it is heavy; conjure with them, Brutus will start a spirit as soon as Caesar: **Now, in the names of all the gods at once, upon what meat doth this our Caesar feed, that he has grown so great?...".**

"O, you and I have heard our fathers say, there was a Brutus once that would have brooked the eternal devil to keep his state in Rome as easily as a king...."

Cassius: (Aside) **"Caesar doth bear me hard; but he loves Brutus: If I were Brutus now and he were Cassius, he should not humor me..."**

The idealist in Brutus in "Julius Caesar"

Brutus, Cassius and other agree that Caesar should be murdered.

Brutus: "Give me your hands all over, one by one."

Cassius: **"And let us swear our resolution."**

Brutus: **"No, not an oath: if not the face of men, the sufferance of our souls, the time's abuse – if these be motives weak, break off betimes, and every man hence to his idle bed..."**

"Swear priests and cowards and men cautelous, old feeble carrions and such suffering souls that welcome wrongs; unto bad causes swear such creatures as men doubt; but do not stain the even virtue of our enterprise, nor the insuppressive mettle of our spirits; to think that or our cause or our performance did need an oath; when every drop of blood that every Roman bears, and nobly bears, is guilty of a several bastardy, if he do break the smallest particle of any promise that hath passed from him."

The absence of malice in Brutus.

Brutus: .. "And, gentle friends, let's kill him boldly, but not wrathfully; let's carve him as dish fit for the gods, not hew him as a carcass fit for hounds:.. This shall make our purpose necessary and not envious: which so appearing to the common eyes, we shall be called purgers, not murderers."

Brutus's righteous indignation in "Julius Caesar."

Brutus: You have done that you should be sorry for. There is no terror, Cassius in your threats, for I am armed so strong in honesty that they pass by me as the idle wind which I respect not. I did send to you for certain sums of gold, which you denied me: **For I can raise no money by vile means:** By heaven, I had rather coin my heart and drop my blood for drachmas, than to wring from the hard hands of peasants their vile trash by any indirection. I did send to you for gold to pay my legions, which you denied me: was that done like Cassius? Should I have answered Caius Cassius so? **When Marcus Brutus grows so covetous to lock such rascal counters from his friends, be ready, gods, with all your thunderbolts; dash him to pieces.**

The arrogance of Caesar in "Julius Caesar."

Caesar: "Cowards die many times before their deaths; the valiant never taste of death but once. Of all the wonders that I have heard, it seems to me most strange that men should fear; seeing that death, a necessary end, will come when it will come."

The servant brings message that the augurers advise that Caesar should not go to the senate.

Caesar: "The gods do this in shame of cowardice: Caesar should be a beast without a heart, if he should stay at home to-day for fear. No, Caesar shall not: **danger knows full well that Caesar is more dangerous than he: We are two lions littered in one day, and I the elder and more terrible: And Caesar shall go forth."**

When Calpurnia begs of Caesar to stay he relents. "Mark Antony shall say I am not well: And, for thy humor, I will stay at home.

Caesar: "..tell them that I will not come to-day: Cannot, is false, and that I dare not, falser: I will not come to-day: tell them so Decius.

Calpurnia: Say he is sick.

Caesar: **Shall Caesar send a lie? Have I in conquest stretched mine arm so far, to be afeard to tell graybeards the truth? Decius, go tell them Caesar will not come.**

Decius: Most mighty Caesar, let me know some cause, lest I be laughed at when I tell them so.

Caesar: **The cause is in my will: I will not come. That is enough to satisfy the senate.**

The astute orator in Mark Antony in "Julius Caesar."

Mark Antony has given an undertaking to Brutus and the other conspirators that he would not speak ill of them. And yet he wants to revenge the murder of Caesar. We see here Mark Antony very cleverly achieving his goal of revenge and yet keeping his promise to the conspirators.

"Come I to speak in Caesar's funeral. He was my friend, faithful and just to me. **But Brutus says he was ambitious; and Brutus is an honorable man.** He hath brought many captives home to

Rome, whose ransoms did the general coffers fill: Did this in Caesar seem ambitious? When that the poor have cried, Caesar hath wept: Ambition should be made of sterner stuff: **Yet Brutus says he was ambitious; And Brutus is an honorable man.** You all did see that on the Lupercal I thrice presented him a kingly crown, which he did thrice refuse: was this ambition? **Yet Brutus says he was ambitious, and, sure, he is an honorable man."**

He resorts to theatrics:

"Bear with me; my heart is in the coffin there with Caesar, and I must pause till it come back to me."

Antony then hints as to what he expects of the mob and yet keep his promise to Brutus.

"O masters, if I were disposed to stir your hearts and minds to mutiny and rage, I should do **Brutus wrong, and Cassius wrong, who, you all know, are honorable men. I will not do them wrong"**

He very tactfully introduces the topic of Caesar's will. He suggests what they should do although not directly.

"But here is a parchment with the seal of Caesar; I found it in his closet, 'tis his will:… which, pardon me, I do not mean to read – and they would go and kiss dead Caesar's wounds, and dip their napkins in his sacred blood, yeg, beg a hair of him for memory, and, dying, mention it within their wills, bequeathing it as a rich legacy unto their issue."

He proceeds to suggest to them what they should exactly do all the while maintaining the façade of loyalty to the conspirators;

"Good friends, sweet friends, let me not stir you up to such a sudden flood of mutiny. They that have done this deed are honorable:

Mark Antony gets exactly the reaction he wants from the mob:

All: We'll mutiny.

First citizen: We'll burn the house of Brutus.

Third citizen: Away, then: come, seek the conspirators.

Mark Anthony magnanimous in victory in "Julius Caesar."

This is what he says of Brutus on his death and defeat in battle.

This was the noblest Roman of them all: All the conspirators save only he did that they did in envy of great Caesar; He only, in a general honest thought and common good to all, made one of them. **His life was gentle, and the elements so mixed in him that Nature might stand up, and say to all the world 'This was a man'**

Macbeth tormented and torn between his ambition to become king and the need to kill Duncan his cousin to achieve his goal.

He's here in double trust ; First, as I am his kinsman and his subject, strong both against the deed; then, as his host, who should against his murderer shut the door, not bear the knife myself. Besides, this Duncan hath borne his faculties so meek, hath been so clear in his great office, that his virtues will plead like angels, trumpet-tongued, against the deep damnation of his taking-off; and pity, like a naked new-born babe, striding the blast, or heaven's cherubim, horsed upon the sightless couriers of the air, shall blow the horrid deed in every eye, that tears shall drown the wind. I have no spur to prick the sides of my intent, **but only vaulting ambition, which overleaps itself and falls on the other.**

Octavius Caesar on Antony whom he fought and defeated:

O Antony; I have followed thee to this; but we do lance diseases in our bodies: I must perforce have shown to thee such a declining day, or look on thine; we could not stall together in the whole world: but yet let me lament, with tears as sovereign as the blood of hearts, **that thou, my brother,** my competitor in top of all design,

my mate in empire, friend and companion in the front of war, the arm of mine own body, and the heart where mine his thoughts did kindle, - that our stars; unreconciliable, should divide our equalness to this.

William Shakespeare.
A BACKGROUND CHECK.

Born in 1564 in Stratford – On – Avon - and died at the age of 52 (1616)

He left a village grammar school at the age of sixteen. He did not attend a university. Stratford at this time had no university.

He was one of eight children.

He was married to Anne Hathaway, eight years his senior.

1585- 1592 for a period of seven years nothing of his life is recorded.

He wrote his first play in 1590, Henry V1 Part 11, at the age of twenty six.

His last play, The Tempest was written in 1611 at the age of forty seven.

Shakespeare wrote in all thirty six plays, one hundred and fifty four sonnets and four poems.

Candidates proposed for the author of his plays are:

Francis Bacon; Edward de Vere, Earl of Oxford.; Christopher Marlowe; Queen Elizabeth.

In 1623 Shakespeare's plays were for the first time put together and in print, known as "The Folio"

He had two daughters, Susanna and Judith and a son, Hamnet.

With the death of his Grand Daughter, Elizabeth (Lady Elizabeth Bernard) sine prole (issueless)

The line of direct descendants of William Shakespeare ended.

The world's number one writer's burial was registered thus.

April 25, Will Shakespeare gent.